Time after time I've tried to let you go, but it's so hard when you are all I want to know.

Can you hear my heart beat? It makes a sound that's incomplete. Since the day you walked into my life, I found that someone who makes me laugh and cry.

You are so sweet it's hard to ignore, your smile is something I simply adore. I wish I didn't feel this way about you, because I feel so lost without you.

As the day goes by, we carry on longing for one another, not knowing when we'll see again the face of the other.

I'm lost for words with nothing left to say, I guess I'll just be on my way. Deleting me has made it clear that you no longer wish to hear me in your ear. You've changed my life and made me see, that no one will understand or know me better than me.

___Dedication___

I would like to start by Thanking
and dedicating this book to God. It
was God who opened my heart and
my eyes to be able to see and feel
each situation that inspired me to
write. For it was God who made it
possible for me to change into the
person I am today. Every step
along the way God was there
speaking through me during all my
days of struggles or my days of joy,
creating and transforming me in to
the being I am and supposed to be.
Thank You God for your love. I love
you and I dedicate and live my life
just for you!

<u>Spiritual Awakening through Poetry</u>

Do you feel what I feel, my soul tells me what we have is real, that you were sent from the heavens above, to teach me how to really Love.

Will you make the time to see, how much you really mean to me? I'll hold you tight throughout the night while the angels bless us with hope and light. They'll keep us strong and holding on for they know that our love is the greatest bond.

I can feel you thinking about me, you want to give me what I truly need. I've changed your life and made you see that your greatest love was you and me. Every day brings a new day for you to see and become the man you desire to be.

My Love for you will never stray, even if you continue to push me away. Though there are times I seem insincere my heart holds you so tight my dear.

The only way to your success is through God, the only way to God is through your heart.

I feel your soul with every breath; I feel your lips upon my neck. When our hands are put together, I feel like we can last forever. My love for you will always be true; I'm waiting for the days these arms get to hold you.

My Light is my Love, My strength is my hope, My heart is my Faith. With these three I will create a new way on Earth as it is in Heaven.

God has given us this day, to show us the light to find our way. May you be blessed to see the truth that God is inside of all you do.

God has a plan for what we should be, it's written on our hands to see. If we follow that path to a T, God will give us our Victory.

If you just laugh, love will find you.

It is said that Jesus died for our sins. So why do you think that it's ok to continue sinning knowing that it's wrong. It's time to take a look at our beliefs and character to see who we really are and who God wants us to be. And only there will we find the answer.

Jesus come walk with me, take me for a ride. Jesus come talk to me, show me the other side.

Your Love was there right from the start, your Love was there holding my heart.

Love has no boundaries, only destinations.

I put my heart on the line and all you did was waste my time. It made me feel like I was weak and I needed you for my heart to beat. Each day that went by I waited for you, wondering if I would be the one you choose.

There's so much that I want to say, but my mind starts trippin and goes astray. All I want to do is hold you tight and caress your body through-out the night. I can feel you deep in my soul, even when I try to let you go.

To see Beauty in that, which is imperfect, is to have the vision of God.

Hello again how time flies, I must say I do miss the butterflies. When I can feel your soul with mine; it feels like a thousand days of pure sunshine.

We'll always be connected deep within our soul, so whenever you are looking for me, that is the place you should go.

Love the ones that are loyal to you, Cherish the ones who adore you.

Through all life's experiences it has taught me how to stand on my own and do things my way.

In life's lessons it's not our stumbles that defines and shape us. It's how we handle the trips and falls that make us who we are.

As each day goes by and you're not by my side, my heart starts to break and I just want to cry. No one else makes me feel this way, even though there has been a few to make me stray. I always come back wanting you more, because your soul is something I need to explore. I know with you I'll be complete, I'm just waiting for you to open up and see. My love is always there holding you tight, shining on you through the lonely nights.

Sometimes uttering those words that one dares not to say is necessary to bring the changes needed to live day to day. In the moment is where you'll find the light, so once you see the stars always keep them in sight.

When we live by the true essence of our soul, that's when we start living and become alive.

Love is a friendship that helps to create inspiring music.

My heart feels cold when you're not near, then tears start to fall because my heart has been speared. You're the one that makes me feel this way, I don't know what to do but run away. You told me that you loved me and I know that it's true, but the hardest thing for me is to know that I love you too. No matter what you do, just know that I will be right here waiting for you.

Forgiveness isn't just for the ones that we love. It's meant to teach the world how to really love, To open up your heart and your mind too; to show you that the world is more than just being about you. It shows us that life is the greatest experience we have, one day we could be happy, next day sad. So take life with all the treasures it holds and keep on trucking down the yellow brick road.

Sometimes we get so caught up in the emotions of who we were and the expectations of others, that we forget to be who we are. The expressway to heaven is to know thy self. To neglect who we are, is to neglect God. For God made us in the likeness of him. To cherish you is to Cherish God. Enjoy the love of being you. Others may not like it, but you came here to live your own life and not theirs. Smile, laugh and Love whomever you desire, for those are gifts from God. Don't let anyone take those from you.

Do you know what it's like to have a mind for yourself? To love someone regardless of wealth, to share the joys life may give, to understand what it means to truly live, to walk this world knowing your fate; while being surrounded by so much hate. Where no one wants to see you succeed, because they are too scared to follow their dreams. Take the time to inspire someone today and put a beautiful smile upon their face.

With all this pain inside of me, I sit and wonder life's mysteries. Should I be still and watch the weak, or take a stand and lead the meek.

Forever love you know what it is, it's the kind that last till the very end. It's the one that makes you move your feet and makes your heart skip a beat.

You and I we're one in the same, that's why I don't want to play no games. God told me that you were the one to help me feel the beat of his drum. So I ask you one thing, let me be the one that you choose.

If you always follow your heart you will come out on top.

Why do we push people away, when we really want for them to stay? Why do we do the things that we do, just to walk a mile in someone else's shoes? Why do we continue to show that we care, when it's obvious that others don't want us there. Why do we love unconditionally hoping it will make us a better being? Life is a grand and beautiful thing if we would learn how to take the pleasures with pain.

God's Love is greater than anything, let's pray to unite humanity.

One day we'll wake up and change the things we never thought would leave our scene. As we go about our day remember that life begins when we are no longer a slave and we start living life in our own unique way.

Be the person you know you are to be, Love yourself unconditionally. Show the world you are the greatest being.

There comes a time in your life when you have to let everything go, so that you may retain the information that will apply to you today.

We are all spiritually connected in one way or another. Whether through an experience in this life or an experience in a past one and for some it's both. Every experience has a consequence whether good or bad, but that is to one's own interpretation. Since no two people are the same, there is no way to determine what is good or bad for one another. What may be good for one may not be good for another. Every person is unique with their own personal power. Some may be similar, but they will never be the same.

Those who try to hide away are the first to fall and go astray. So tell the truth in all you do, so only good will come to you. Lead a life of truth and love and the lord will bless you from the kingdom above. Open your eyes to all you see and bless the ones who are really in need.

Fear will bring your spirit down, fear will put you in the ground, fear will take what you thought was yours, Fear will close your open doors. Faith will lift you to your best, Faith will help you through any test, Faith is what you need to be, one with God for eternity.

Sometimes we just wake up and realize that we are the ones that put our self in chains. We realize that our actions, Behaviors or lack of, are the reason we feel the way we do or the reason we are in situations that are causing us disappointment. The only way to get things to change is to make them change. You and only you control your future. So if you want it go get it.

Perfection is; knowing that everything in your life has purpose. Purpose is what makes life worth living for. Every person place or thing in this world is a key to helping you achieve your perfection. Know that no one can define your life but you, and no one will completely understand your purpose but you and God. They will however appreciate you and all you do. So make sure you do the best you know how to.

Love is the greatest power on Earth, it's something that most experience from the day of birth. So love your life and all that's in it, for there will come a time when you will no longer be in it. The seasons are changing, the world is creating, and things are blossoming into something new. Everything will change, nothing remains the same. So love all things that come to you..

Sometimes Love is meant for a season, sometimes love has a reason. Sometimes love is to help us grow, sometimes love just needs to be let go. Sometimes love will cause you pain, sometime love will bring you change. Sometimes love will wipe your tears, sometimes love will last for years. Always remember to keep your faith and continue to love as the seasons change, God will bless you in all that you do. Just always remember to keep loving you.

Blessed is the person who follows their heart, for they know where they are going right from the start. Blessed will be you if you do the same, for we all came here to play this game. Everyone you meet is fated you see, you choose them to help you gain your victory. One wrong move and you could lose, so be wise when you chose your every move. We came here to win, not to lose so play your part in all that you do.

Some of us are more special than others you see, but that doesn't make us better than thee. God has chosen us to fight, because we are his godly knights. Inside your heart you know who you are, so keep on shining like a shooting star. Always remember that you are love and God sent you here to show the world how to truly love.

One of the hardest things in life is to tell someone you love goodbye. Even if it's not forever you'll miss the moment of you together, For every memory that you shared is something that you could never compare. Love is something that will never fade; we just show it in a different way. Be blessed as you go about your life and know that everything is going to be alright.

You are the light that helps me shine; your love makes me feel like I've had too much wine. When I look into your eyes, it has me feeling so alive. I get chills up my spine, while I sit here dreaming wishing you were mine. You've got such a hold on me, like our love will last for eternity. Thank You God for sending love my way, and showing me you're there in your special way. Your love is something I cannot deny, because you are the greatest sunshine.

You are the breath that feeds my soul; you're the other half that makes me whole. You are the one God chose for me; you are the one who will fulfill my dreams. When I first met you I was hooked, like a school nerd reading a really good book. I knew one day I'd have to make you mine, I didn't realize it would take some time. Either way I'm here to stay, so wrap me up and carry me away. May God be with you in all that you do, and always remember that I do Love you...

Summer has finally come to an end. Autumn is here changing leaves again. The mist of romance is in the air, we all are longing for someone who truly cares. It's that time when we want someone to hold us tight and kiss us passionately throughout the night. Someone to walk with us along the beach and share our dreams we haven't reached; someone who will love us just as we are; someone who will catch our shooting star. So fall in love under the moonlight today and you'll create a love that will always remain. Welcome to autumn and all that's in store, love

is the greatest thing this season
that will knock at your door.

The autumns mist upon my face,
God's love shown by beautiful
grace. My soul was saved from this
earthly placed because I fought to
follow my faith. Heaven has
opened and let me in, to save me
from all of sin. I have followed my
path that was meant to be, even
threw the pain and misery. Every
step I took had given me life, to
bring me back and make me right.
For I belong to God you see, I am
the soldier of Love, Judgment and
Prosperity. No wicked deed will
keep me from the job on earth that

needs to be done. So follow your heart and not your mind and you will come out shining right on time.

To love someone will the essence of all your soul and watch them walk away with someone else is the ultimate blessing, because at some point you will learn the value of true unconditional love; which is to let go and let it flow. Love has no boundaries only destinations. Love is not meant to be controlled; love is a free spirit and should be treated just as it is.

Today will be a day filled with Love and Peace, with desires to have more than the finer things; A day where you'll want to cherish the one that you're thinking of and shower them with the gift of unconditional love. So make every effort to express how you feel and never let anyone tell you that it isn't real. Smile as you go about your day and know the Goddess of love is shining on you today.

There were some people born in this life to be alone, not because they are un-deserving of a marriage, but because they are more beneficial to society if their spirit remains pure. Celibacy is not about being obedient to God, It's meant to keep a person pure. That way they can use the energy they were born with to make their mark in this world.

Loyalty is so hard to find when there are so many people playing with minds. Promising things that will never be, taking advantage of the thing they see. People hoping one day they'll live their dreams, while others sit around plotting how to scheme. So when you find someone you can trust, hold them close for it's a must. You never know who they might be, maybe an angel sent to set you free.

When you find that which brings your soul pure happiness, never let it go. When our soul is happy nothing else matters, for anything that we desire is manifested through the happiness of our soul. Happiness is the key to all that we dream. It holds the power to all that is unseen. So if you want to be a greater being, never give up on that in which you dream.

Rise and shine to a beautiful day, thank God for showing you the right way. Blessed is the person who follows their heart, for they know where they are going right from the start. For no one else knows where you've been, and no one else can feel your heart from within, no one can love you better than you and no one else could ever fill your shoes. You are special in every way, so take time to thank God for making you this way.

Why does life turn us around with every change of a sound? With every breath that we speak, our minds are changing rapidly. Hoping to mold us into who we are, while we sit and wish upon a star; forgetting the mistakes that we've made; so that we can make tomorrow a brighter day. Loving each other unconditionally and uniting as one to create the world's brightest light beam.

True love will come, true love will go but the love of God will always hold. So let go of expectations and start anew or you'll lose out on what God has planned for you. Be brave, be wise and always remember to follow your heart.

To have a successful marriage one must have an understanding and acceptance to the meaning of it, which is; Making A Righteous Redemption In Accepting God Eternally. Once you have done that, success is yours.

Today is a day to purify and be filled with so much joy that the world comes alive. To think of others before yourself, to not show regards to any wealth. To love thy neighbors like thy self, to help the ones who need your help.

One of the most amazing things in this world is being true to you. When you are true to yourself, you are true to everyone else. In truth we are set free and we live in peace. We learn to live without expectations and all the weight of the world. Be who you truly are and watch your world blossom before your very eyes.

As I sit alone eating today, I watch the people and start to pray. Even though they have someone near they're filled with loneliness and plagued by fear. They sit with smiles upon their face, hoping they're masking the pain that remains. If they only knew that they could be free, by breaking the chains that causes the grief...

Take it back into time; remember the essence of when you were nine. You could be anything you wanted to be, the sky was the limit it was endlessly. You knew exactly who you wanted to be, you lived everyday trying to follow that dream. But somewhere along the way you lost that sight, you took a chance on another flight. It brought you safely here today, but your heart is ready to go the other way. It's time to let go of all the fear and be the one thing that brought you here.

When you find the existence of your souls being, stand in the sun and watch it gleam. A full moon can bring such beautiful things, when you open up your heart and let it sing. Be patient with all the things you do and remember that heaven is counting on you.

Fight for what you know is true; love the ones who really love you. Walk with faith for every step; count your blessings for every breath. Believe in your heart and what you stand for, and always remember to walk through heavens doors.

At times we are so caught up in the emotions of things going on that we forget to thank God for giving us today to make a difference in our life or someone else's. If you woke up breathing today than you are blessed, you have the gift of life and should be thankful for every moment. Blessed is the person who understands and values life.

It is hard to understand someone/something when you put it into a category it does not belong in. There are some people/things that are meant to be free, flowing like the wind and not categorized. Putting limitations on them/it hinders growth. If you have an understanding that everything that is done is for the betterment of everyone, then you realize that you have the understanding that you need.

Some people think that the heart is tainted; that it deceives us, because it can lead us into directions that we later perceive as not so good. However, in reality had we not experienced those situations then we would not have been able to grow from them. When we follow our heart, it helps us grow into the person we desire to be. When we follow our mind, we end up losing time and we become further away from the person we desire to be. It's time to stop being what others want you to be; free yourself and follow your dreams.

When you spend time with God you receive clarity on the situations in your life. Sometimes regardless of how much you love someone or something you have to let them or it go, so that you can flourish into a better person than you have ever imagined. Change is necessary to grow and prosper. May God be with you in all you do.

There is so much beauty in the world that we fail to see, because we are all caught up in the lives that we lead. We start chasing things that were never meant to be, which causes us to change our destiny. Life is so simple if you chose it to be, just follow your heart and believe in your dreams. God gave us the greatest gift on earth you see, to love everyone unconditionally. So when you see someone down and out, take the time to help them out. Be the person you want to be, because that is your greatest Victory.

All they see is a beautiful face; they don't see the memories that have been erased. They sit and think I have it all, not knowing how many times I had to fall. They don't know that my heart has been broken, because people used me like a token. All they see is what they want it to be, because their hearts are filled with so much greed. I cry myself to sleep wishing upon the stars, hoping they'll take away all my pains and scars. Never let anyone define who you are, keep God's peace and you'll go far..

Sometimes we take life for granted and we overlook those whose life is un-planted. All it takes is a minute or two to help someone back into their shoes. It's so easy for us to get off track, but it takes much longer to get us back. So as you go about your day, help someone along their way. Be the Angel they are looking for to help them get to Heavens door.

I'm trying to hold on to your love, but it's fading away like a blue dove. My mind is telling me to let you go, but my heart keeps saying just to go slow. Why do I have to feel so torn? Maybe it's because I've just been reborn. There are so many things going crazy in my life, but when I think of you everything starts to go right. I want to leave and run away with you, but I'm scared of what others might think and do. So I'll sit here and pretend that I'm ok even though my heart is broken in so many ways.

I can't even begin to describe just how you make my soul come alive. Even at the thought of you, it sends my heart soaring straight to the moon. The sound of your voice makes me so weak that I lose all control and the ability to speak. My knees start to shake when you hold me tight, so you grip me closer with all your might. Being with you seems like heaven you see, everything is so blissfully. There is no way I'd let you go, because this feeling was always meant to flow.

Blessings come in all forms. Sometimes they are as simple as listening to someone share their excitement and passions with you. There are also times when the greatest joys in our life are inspired by a person's smile. So make sure that you live, love, laugh and smile every day, for you never know whose life you may change

Sometimes in life we fail to see, the beauty in people we happen to meet. We get so caught up in our worldly things, that it changes our perception and the way we think. Then it takes time to humble ourselves and get us back to our spiritual health. But all we need to do to achieve this peace, is pray to God to change our scene.

Dreams are visions from our soul. Whether they are from this life or a past one, they are something that has or will awaken your sole purpose. Sometimes you just need to let go of everything and only pursue that which fully satisfies you, knowing that everything will be just fine. For God will Bless those who do not fear their future and embrace the unknowing with open arms. "Dreams were meant to be pursued."

Everyone wants a love where they don't have to hide, those beautiful feelings deep inside. Someone who loves you just as you are, someone who doesn't sway even when you are far. Someone who knows exactly what it is you need and cherishes the moments they watch you sleep. Someone who kisses you softly with a little bit of bite and holds you close through every night. Someone who is not afraid to stand up and fight, just so they can keep you right by their side. So when you find the one who does all these things, open up your heart and let it sing. Thank God for such a beautiful thing and honor your Love over everything.

There are times when we wake up and realize the veil that has been blocking us, has been lifted and we see life for what it really is. We understand the journey of love never ends. Every day is a new day in which we find love in the people we meet, the trees as they blow in the wind, the journeys we take with friends and the existence in just being able to live, laugh and breathe. Love is an essence that never goes away; it should be the focus of each and every day. There is no such thing as life without love, for life is Love. Capture the essence of love today and your life will be better in every way.

Rain, Rain, Rain. I'm falling slowly and I don't want to look back. For the first time I feel like I'm on the right track. All I see is the light straight ahead, as I brush my lips gently across your head. When you are lying next to me, I become lost in a beautiful dream. I wonder if this will last forever, or is it just for the moment that we are together. Your love has me flying so high in the clouds; nothing can reach me to bring me down. Peace is where I

*want us to be, so let's run away
and follow our dreams...*

*Sometimes love is so unexpected, it
will wrap you up close if you chose
to let it. It will cover your soul with
a joyful bliss; it will tingle like
butterflies with every kiss. It will
wipe away everything you use to
miss and it will help you grant your
every wish. So if love happens to
come your way, continue to
nurture it every day. It will blossom
you into someone new, a person
this world could really look up to.*

Life is meant for us to live and be free, not to hide secrets and dwell in our greed. It's not meant for us to conform to the ways of others, or disrespect and lie to our mother's, father's, sister's or brothers. Honesty and freedom starts from within, and then it will spread like a wildfire caught in the wind. Know yourself if you want to be free and stop hiding away because others do not agree. Be the greatest you know you can be and God will bless you with everything.

Strength comes from knowing your weaknesses and triumphing over your obstacles. Wisdom comes from learning your lessons and preparing for what is yet to come. Independence is what you gain when you fight for what you want, while refusing to give up; which then results in conquering your dreams. Be strong, Be Wise, Be Brave!

Life gives us each moment to seize the opportunities that come our way. All it takes is the courage to persevere over the obstacles that try to get us to sway. Our lives are what we create them to be, so keep going towards your Beautiful dreams. Everything will happen if you continue to believe. Victory is the only thing you should see.

When we think that we have it all figured out, we realize that we do not. Every moment of each day things are changing. Life is about evolving into something greater than we were the moment before. Yesterday is gone, tomorrow has not yet arrived and today we can find ourselves full of life. Greatness comes from having an understanding of Truth, Love and passion, which then will lead us to Peace and Happiness.

Open up your eyes, your ears and your heart to the energy that surrounds you. It is speaking to you through everything that comes your way. It is pointing you to the path that you were meant to be on. So if you learn to just let it flow, it will grab a hold and take you where you want to go.

Beauty is not described by what we see; it is the essence of something in all living things. It is something that makes us feel so good, like when we make a sacrifice because we could. Life isn't always as easy as we want it to be, but it will flow so much better when we're not focused on me. If we learn to put others before ourselves, we find we don't need anything else.

Compassion is one of the things we need in this life, to help us push forward through all of the strife. Be blessed each and every day and love others as you do yourself in every way.

Smile and know that life is Grand, then let it take you by the hand. Let it show you a place unknown, a place where you will never be alone. Be happy as you go about your way and enjoy the essence of every day.

Fight for what you know is true; love the ones who really love you. Walk with faith for every step; count your blessings for every breath. Believe in your heart and what you stand for, and always remember to walk through heavens doors.

Some of us have been on Earth before and we know the secrets and powers that life has in store. If we use them for our greed; instead of helping those in need, Our consequences will be greater than we've ever seen. There are reasons why we need to come together, so that our spirit may live in peace forever. Don't get caught up in the worldly things, remember who you are and what you came to show human beings. There is a God inside of you, let it flow and create you anew.

Some people will fight the things they see, because their heart is not where it used to be. They think they are who they were before, but God came in and closed that door. No need to debate with someone who is not as wise as you, for it has taken you a long time to get into your shoes. Be grateful that you've grown from there and continue to shed God's light everywhere. God Bless you on this very day and May miracles shine upon you in every way.

Today was the day I was made anew. I was taught by God to understand everything I do. I was given a chance to make something right and I went from a caterpillar to a butterfly. Peace is what you've brought to me and that is worth more than any diamond ring. Thank You God for leading my way, for in your Love is where I want to always stay..

I want to thank you for taking the time to read God's words. May these words shed light in to your life the way they have in mine. In our life Journey some things are not always clear and it feels good to know that God is there every step of the way guiding us, even when we do not realize it. I share these words with you today, in hope that they help you along your way. God Bless Every one of you, and I look forward to continuing to share my experiences and wisdom with all of you...